45 P

The Young World Library is a series designed for the young reader. The stories are taken from some of the world's best-known novels, plays, legends, operas and ballets. They have been simplified and re-told in a way which keeps close to the spirit of the original, while bringing everything within the immediate grasp of the young reader's understanding of words. Equally important are the illustrations, which have been chosen both to delight the eye and to match the special character of each story. Thus the Young World Library offers young readers a unique stepping stone towards the use and enjoyment of books. It also introduces them in a lively, up-to-date way to many famous stories and characters from the wonderful world of literature and the performing arts.

Series Editor: Alan Blackwood

Cover design by Hildegarde Bone

S.B.N. 72380959 3
Printed in Great Britain by A. Wheaton & Co., Exeter

THE WOODEN HORSE OF TROY

Adapted and told by
Alan Blackwood

Illustrated by
Denis Manton

Based on the epic poems *The Iliad* by Homer
and *The Aeneid* by Virgil

Long, long ago there lived a beautiful Greek princess whose name was Helen. She was so beautiful that some people said she was the daughter of Zeus, the chief of all the gods. Others said she was the daughter of a beautiful, graceful swan.

Helen was married to the handsome Prince Menelaus, and they lived happily together in a palace by the sea. But soon their happiness was to end.

For one day, another young prince arrived at the palace. His name was Paris, and he had sailed over the sea from the famous city of Troy. People had told him about Helen and how beautiful she was, and he wanted to see her for himself.

Indeed, Helen was even more beautiful than Paris had imagined, and he fell in love with her at once. So one night he carried her off to his ship and set sail again for Troy.

When Prince Menelaus found out what had happened, he was beside himself with grief and rage. He called all the other Greek kings and princes to his palace.

"Fellow Greeks," he said, "Prince Paris of Troy has stolen from me my beloved wife Helen. Will you help me to win her back again?"

"Aye, we will," the other Greek kings and princes replied.

"Very well, then," Prince Menelaus continued. "Let us build a great fleet of galley ships, so that we can sail across the sea, destroy the city of Troy and rescue Helen."

While the fleet was being built, the Greek kings and princes collected a great army together. Prince Menelaus also asked Achilles and Odysseus, two of the bravest and most skilful warriors in all Greece, to go with them. Then, when the galley ships were ready, and the wind blew fair and strong, they all set sail for Troy. "With our wonderful fleet and our great army, and with brave Achilles and Odysseus to help us, we shall soon conquer Troy," Prince Menelaus declared.

But Troy was a mighty city. It stood upon a steep hill, and was surrounded by the strongest and highest walls that had ever been built. And it also had many brave warriors to defend it, including the valiant Hector. All the galley ships and all the armies in the world would not find it easy to conquer such a city.

Thus it was that when the Greek armies arrived before the walls of Troy, the fighting went on for many months. Sometimes the Greek soldiers advanced on the city and almost managed to climb over one of the walls. Then the Trojan soldiers would beat them back again. Both sides had so many brave soldiers that no one could tell who would win the war.

One day Achilles met Hector in battle. "Oh, Achilles," Hector cried. "You have not long to live, for my spear shall pierce your heart."

"It shall not," Achilles replied. "For my shield was forged by Hephaestus, blacksmith of the gods, and it will protect me forever."

Achilles was right. Hector threw his spear with all his strength and skill. But though it buried itself deep in Achilles' shield, Achilles himself was not harmed.

Then Achilles ran at Hector with his sword, and with one great blow struck him down and killed him. For weeks afterwards the Trojan people mourned the death of their hero, Hector. "Hector's death has made the Trojans weep instead of fight," Prince Menelaus observed. "Soon they will surrender, and we shall rescue Helen."

But the Trojans still did not surrender, and the Greek armies still could not get past the thick, high walls of the city. Even Achilles wondered if they could ever win.

At last Odysseus called the Greek kings and princes together. "Comrades," he told them, "I think I know how to get inside this mighty city of Troy. I shall build a wooden horse."

"A wooden horse?" Prince Menelaus asked. "If we cannot defeat the Trojans with spears and swords, how can we beat them with a wooden horse?"

"Be patient," Odysseus replied, "and I will show you."

Odysseus then told them that his wooden horse would be large enough for soldiers to hide in. "That is the most important part of my plan," he said. "Leave the rest to me."

Odysseus told his soldiers how to build the giant wooden horse, and when it was finished, he asked Achilles to climb inside with him. "Tonight," he told the rest of his soldiers, "I want you to leave the wooden horse outside the walls of Troy, close to the main gate. Then go away and hide. But be ready with your swords and spears. For when you hear my trumpet sound, you must attack at once!"

That night, in the darkness, the great wooden horse was pulled up the hill and left outside the main gate of Troy. And next morning, as the first rays of the sun brightened the sky, there it was for all to see. "Look there!" a Trojan guard called out to his comrades. "What kind of a horse is that? Sound the alarm!"

Then all the people of Troy climbed the walls to see the marvellous wooden horse. Paris was there too. "The Greek armies have fled in the night," he declared. "The wooden horse is a gift of the gods, to reward us for our victory. Open the gate and bring the wooden horse inside. Perhaps it is filled with treasure!"

So the Trojans opened the gate and pulled the wooden horse into the city.

All day they walked round and round the horse, but could find out nothing more about it.

Then, when it grew dark again, and the Trojans had all gone to sleep, Odysseus and Achilles opened the secret door in the belly of the horse and dropped quietly to the ground. They had been inside the whole time. Silently they crept up to the gate of the city and opened it wide. Then Odysseus stood between the pillars of the gate. He placed his long silver trumpet to his lips and blew one long, high note.

The Trojans nearly jumped out of their skins when they heard the trumpet. Some of them ran to the gate and tried to close it again. But Odysseus and Achilles fought them off, while the other Greek warriors rushed up the hill from their hiding places. "This way," Odysseus cried, as more warriors came running up the hill. "The gate of Troy is open wide. The high stone walls cannot stop us now!"

The Greek soldiers ran through the streets of Troy with flaming torches. They set fire to the buildings as they ran, until Troy was burning from end to end.

Prince Menelaus led the way to the palace where Paris held Helen captive. Paris drew his sword when he saw the prince running up the palace steps.

"Your sword cannot protect you from my anger," Prince Menelaus cried. "For stealing from me my beloved wife, you shall die." And so saying, he slew Paris with his spear.

When Prince Menelaus found the beautiful Helen, he brought her to the steps of the palace where the victorious Greek warriors had gathered. "Soldiers and heroes of Greece," he declared. "Thanks to Odysseus and his wonderful wooden horse, we have been able to conquer the great city of Troy. The Trojans have fled. Paris has been killed. And here is our beautiful Princess Helen, whom we have fought so long and so hard to rescue."

Prince Menelaus had a galley ship specially built to carry Helen back over the sea to Greece. It had a golden bow and silver masts. The sails were made of the purest silk, and the oars were made of ivory.

As Helen stepped aboard her ship, a great cheer went up from the Greek armies. It was so loud and long that it was heard right across the sea, so that the people of Greece knew that their beautiful Princess Helen was coming home again.